From Violent to Violet: God Removed the "N"

Sequel to "Only God Can Grow a Violet Out of a Pile of Dirt"

Written by Violet Newborn

Dedication

To my son, Logan, whose love and light have guided me through the darkest of times. You are my constant reminder of God's grace and the beauty that arises from brokenness. This book is for you, so that one day you may understand the depth of my journey and the strength that lies within you too. And to every survivor who has felt unseen and unheard—you are not alone. Your story matters, and I dedicate this work to the power of your healing.

Acknowledgments

First and foremost, I thank God for guiding me through every step of this transformation and for showing me that beauty truly does rise from ashes. Without His grace, none of this would have been possible.

To my family, especially Logan, who has been my inspiration and my reason to continue striving for healing, I am eternally grateful. You remind me every day of the purpose behind this journey.

To the friends and mentors who have walked with me during this process, thank you for your encouragement, prayers, and belief in me when I doubted myself. You were my strength when I needed it most. Special thanks to Maurice Clifton Sr., Raegan Newborn, and Josh Snead for being part of the vision of Color Your Story Onto Mine and for standing beside me in this mission.

To every participant of the Color Your Story Onto Mine workshops who trusted me with your stories and allowed me to share in your healing journey, you have been my greatest teachers. Your courage to open up and express your truth has fueled my own growth and healing.

Finally, a heartfelt thanks to the readers of this book. Your support and willingness to embark on this journey of transformation with me mean more than words can express.

Table of Contents

Foreword

I have known Violet for many years, and witnessing her transformation has been nothing short of miraculous. When I first met her, she was a woman struggling under the weight of immense trauma, navigating life with the pain and scars of her past. Yet, even then, there was a spark—a light that had not been completely extinguished. Through her faith, resilience, and deep commitment to healing, that spark became a fire, and she emerged from her past not just as a survivor, but as a beacon of hope for others.

From Violent to Violet: God Removed the 'N' is a reflection of the incredible work Violet has done, not just in her own life, but in the lives of so many others. Her story is one of redemption and grace, and this book is a powerful testament to the ability of God to transform even the most broken places in our hearts.

I am honored to have witnessed Violet's journey and even more honored to write this foreword for a book that I know will inspire and change lives. This is not just a memoir; it is a roadmap for anyone who is searching for healing, for peace, and for the courage to face their own 'N' traits. As you read these pages, prepare to be moved, challenged, and ultimately, transformed.

Preface

When I first began to write From Violent to Violet, I had no idea how much of myself I would have to pour onto these pages. This book is not just a recount of past events; it is a living reflection of my transformation—a journey that I am still on to this day. I wrote this book because I felt called to share the deeper story behind my healing, not just for myself, but for every person who has been silenced by trauma, violence, and shame.

This book was born out of my personal journey of survival, but it grew into something much bigger. I realized that by sharing my own story, I could create a space for others to find healing too. Through my work with Color Your Story Onto Mine, I've seen firsthand the power of storytelling and artistic expression in the healing process. The more I engaged with survivors, the more I realized that my own transformation was a part of a much larger movement—a movement of healing, empowerment, and reclaiming our voices.

Writing this book has been an act of vulnerability, but it has also been one of empowerment. My prayer is that as you read this book, you will see yourself in these pages. Whether you are a survivor of trauma or simply someone searching for deeper meaning in your life, I hope this story encourages you to embark on your own journey of transformation. God's grace is available to all of us, and I am living proof that no matter how broken we may feel, we can be made whole again.

Thank you for joining me on this journey. May these words bring you hope, healing, and the courage to remove the 'N' in your own life.

— Violet Newborn

Introduction: The Power of Transformation

When I reflect on the journey that brought me here, from darkness to light, I'm reminded of one simple yet profound truth: transformation is possible for all of us. My story, though unique in its details, is not unlike yours or anyone else's who has faced adversity, trauma, and deep pain. This book, From Violent to Violet: God Removed the 'N', is a testimony to the power of transformation—a story of how God turned my life around by removing the destructive traits that once defined me.

The letter "N" became a symbol of the things that held me back: Narcissism, Negativity, and Numbing. These traits, born from years of trauma, abuse, and survival, shaped my worldview and my relationships. I couldn't see beyond the walls I had built around my heart. I was surviving, not living. But survival often comes at a cost, and for me, that cost was my true identity. These "N" traits shielded me from pain, but they also shielded me from love, joy, and connection.

Through God's grace, I began to understand that these traits were not a part of who I truly was; they were a product of my circumstances, a response to the violence I endured. Over time, I learned that I didn't have to live in the shadow of these traits any longer. God began to remove each "N," replacing them with something greater. The process wasn't easy, and it didn't happen overnight, but it was real, and it was transformational. As He stripped away the layers of defense and pain, I realized something beautiful: the "N" was no longer part of me, and in its place was a name I could claim with pride—Violet.

Violet is more than just a name; it's a symbol of the beauty and grace that emerged from the ashes of my pain. The violet flower, delicate yet strong, grows in places where other flowers might not survive. It thrives in adversity, blooming even in the most unlikely conditions. That's how I see myself now. Where there was once violence, there is now Violet—a woman who stands in her truth, not as a victim of her past but as a survivor who has been reborn into something new.

This book is not just a memoir of my journey. It is an invitation for you to witness the process of healing, to see how God can take the most broken parts of us and create something beautiful. It's about removing the traits that no longer serve us, the "N" traits that keep us stuck, and embracing the transformation that awaits on the other side.

As you read through these pages, I hope you see yourself in the story. I hope you find encouragement to remove the "N" traits in your own life—whether they are Narcissism, Negativity, Numbing, or something else entirely. God is ready to transform you too, just as He did for me. We are not meant to live in violence, whether physical, emotional, or spiritual. We are meant to bloom, just like the violet, under the grace and love of our Creator.

This is the story of how God removed the "N" in my life and how I reclaimed the name Violet —a name that now represents beauty, strength, and the power of transformation. Welcome to the journey.

Part I: The Storm of the Past
Chapter 1: Ugly, Stupid, Floozy

In the somber shadows of a crumbling house in Memphis, a girl was born into chaos. Her name was Violet, but no one called her that. Instead, they called her Ugly for the bruises that often colored her skin, Stupid for the slow, thoughtful way she spoke, and Floozy for the attention she never sought but always seemed to attract.

The world Violet came into wasn't kind or gentle. It was a world of sharp edges and darker intentions, where the innocence of a child was something to be scoffed at and stripped away. Violet's mother, a woman as fragile as the glass that often shattered across their living room floor, battled demons that no one else could see. Her schizophrenia painted their dilapidated home with horrors that Violet, even as a child, had to navigate daily.

The most chilling memories for Violet were the flashbacks to her grandfather—a towering figure whose affections twisted into abuses that left her soul as bruised as her body. He called her to his lap with a smile that never reached his eyes and spoke softly with words that slithered like snakes. "You're my special girl," he'd whisper, right before the darkness descended and the pain began. Each encounter left a scar, a mark that Violet learned to hide from the world but never from herself.

The abuse wasn't always hidden. Sometimes, it was starkly public, shamelessly overt. Violet's mother, in the throes of her illness, would strip naked, driven by voices only she could hear. She'd parade down the street, leaving Violet to chase after her, trying to cover her, to shield her from the mocking eyes of their neighbors. These episodes were punctuated by violent outbursts at home, where her mother would turn on Violet, the closest target, with whatever was within reach—a belt, a shoe, a bottle.

School was no refuge. Violet carried the stench of poverty—the musty smell of unwashed clothes and human despair. Her classmates kept their distance, as if misfortune was contagious, and teachers looked on with pity but no intervention. Violet learned early that to survive was to remain invisible, to avoid the notice that brought pain.

Yet, despite the violence that defined her early existence, there were moments of reprieve that hinted at a different life, glimpses of what being loved might feel like. An old woman down the street, Mrs. Jenkins, would sometimes beckon Violet inside her warm, cookie-scented kitchen. There, Violet would receive a smile and a cup of hot chocolate, a contrast so stark to her cold, loveless home that it felt like stepping into a fairy tale. Mrs. Jenkins never asked about the bruises or the fear that flickered behind Violet's eyes; she simply offered a safe haven, a brief escape that Violet cherished deeply.

In the solitude of her room, beneath a loose floorboard, Violet kept a ragged notebook—her secret repository of thoughts and dreams. Here, she wrote not of the ugliness and stupidity others saw in her, but of a world where she was Violet—bright, beautiful, and beloved. She wrote of colors and places that didn't exist in her gray world, of people who spoke kindness and touched gently. Each word was a defiance, a rebellion against the narrative that had been forced upon her.

This notebook became her sanctuary, her way of holding onto the fragile threads of hope that whispered of a different life—a life where she was not Ugly, Stupid, or Floozy, but simply Violet, a girl with a future bright as the colors she wrote about. It was in these written worlds that Violet first dared to believe in the possibility of escape, of transformation. And it was these dreams that would one day fuel her journey from a violent past to a future she alone would shape.

Chapter 2: Numb and Noxious

By the time I was old enough to understand that the world around me was broken, I had already begun to break along with it. The pain, the abuse, the constant barrage of violence—physical, emotional, and sexual—had taken its toll. The only way I knew to survive was to turn off every part of me that felt. I became numb, an empty shell, hollowed out from the inside by the horrors I'd witnessed and the ones that had been inflicted on me.

Numbness, I learned, was a gift. It was the only thing that kept me from being destroyed by the things that happened to me. When my stepbrother would come into my room at night, I would simply close my eyes, hold my breath, and retreat into the darkness of my mind. I didn't cry anymore. I didn't scream. I just waited for it to be over, like it was a chore I had to endure to make it to the next day.

I became so skilled at turning off my emotions that I barely recognized myself anymore. I had no need for happiness or love. Those things didn't exist in my world, and they certainly weren't meant for someone like me. In place of those emotions, I filled myself with numbness and a growing sense of detachment from everything around me.

I was only a child, but I had learned early that feeling nothing was better than feeling everything. I could turn off the pain, the fear, and the shame by disconnecting from it all. I didn't let anyone in, didn't let anyone close enough to hurt me. Not that there was anyone who cared enough to try. My mother was lost in her own world, a haze of madness and violence that kept her a million miles away from me, even when we were in the same room. My father, when he was around, was a silent presence, a ghost in the house who saw everything but said nothing.

The men who came and went, the ones who hurt me, violated me—they were like shadows, fleeting and inconsequential. I couldn't give them the satisfaction of my tears, of my fear. So, I gave them nothing. I was a puppet, an object to be used and discarded. And I let them. It was easier that way.

But while I was numb on the inside, a different kind of darkness started to take root within me. As I learned to survive by disconnecting from my emotions, I also learned how to adapt to the world around me. The violence I had endured—the violence that had shaped me—began to seep into my own behavior. I became noxious, a poison to myself and to anyone who got too close.

If I couldn't feel, then I wouldn't let anyone else feel either. I adopted the very traits I had seen in the people who hurt me: cruelty, manipulation, detachment. I wasn't just surviving anymore—I was becoming something more dangerous. I was becoming violent, not just in the way I interacted with others, but in the way I saw myself. I was at war with my own body, my own soul.

The violence I inflicted on myself was as deliberate as the violence that had been inflicted on me. I would cut myself just to see if I could still feel pain, but even that became hollow. The blood would flow, the wounds would sting, but the numbness would return quickly, swallowing me whole. I learned to crave the pain, not because I wanted to feel alive, but because it was the only thing that reminded me I was still human.

I hated myself, and I hated the world that had made me this way. But there was a strange power in that hatred. It gave me control, a feeling that I had never had before. If I could turn the violence I had experienced into something I could wield, then maybe I could survive a little longer. Maybe I could even thrive in it.

In school, I lashed out at anyone who crossed my path. Other kids were afraid of me, and I liked it that way. I wasn't big, but I was mean. I learned quickly that a sharp tongue and a willingness to use my fists could keep people at a distance. The same way my stepbrother had used violence to control me, I used it to control my surroundings. I couldn't be the victim if I made myself the aggressor.

My teachers labeled me a troublemaker, a lost cause. I was the kid who fought in the hallways, who cursed out the staff, who always seemed to be one breath away from a breakdown. But no one ever asked why. No one wondered what had turned a little girl into a ticking time bomb. To them, I was just a problem to be managed, a statistic in the making.

I stopped going to school as often as I could. It didn't matter. I wasn't learning anything that could help me. What did math or science have to do with surviving the life I had been dealt? What was the point of homework when I could barely make it through the night without another man ripping away pieces of me?

At home, the cycle of abuse continued. My stepbrother's nightly visits were as regular as the sunrise. My mother's schizophrenic episodes became more violent, more unpredictable. And I? I continued to detach. When she would beat me with whatever object was closest—an iron, a frying pan, a belt buckle—I wouldn't flinch. I wouldn't scream. I would go numb, just like I always did.

And yet, despite everything, there was a growing anger inside me, a burning rage that I didn't know how to control. I had spent years learning how to suppress my emotions, how to shut down the parts of myself that felt too deeply. But anger—anger was different. Anger didn't care about numbness. It burned through everything.

That anger, that noxious poison inside me, spilled out in the worst ways. I would lash out at my younger siblings when they annoyed me, hitting them or yelling until they cried. I didn't want to be like my mother, but I could feel myself becoming her. I could feel the violence becoming part of me, something I couldn't stop. It was as if I was destined to be a monster, just like everyone else in my life.

There were days when I would stand in front of the bathroom mirror, staring at my reflection. I didn't recognize the person looking back at me. My eyes were hollow, my skin pale and bruised. I looked like a ghost, a shadow of a girl who had never really existed. I was ugly. I was stupid. I was a floozy. The names they had called me weren't just insults—they were truths, etched into my skin, my mind, my soul.

I was nothing. I was no one.

But deep inside me, buried beneath the numbness, the anger, and the pain, there was still a small, flickering light. It was weak, almost invisible, but it was there. It was the part of me that still wanted to be saved, the part of me that still believed—against all odds—that there was more to life than this.

I didn't know it yet, but that light would be my salvation. It would be the thing that saved me from myself, from the numbness, from the noxious violence that threatened to consume me completely.

But for now, all I could do was survive.

Chapter 3: The Seeds of Violence

Violence wasn't something I chose; it was something that had been planted inside me long before I even understood what it meant. The seeds of violence took root in the soil of my childhood, watered by every cruel word, every unwanted touch, every blow that landed on my small, fragile body. I didn't ask to be this way, but eventually, I learned to embrace it. Violence was all I knew, and in time, it became my only source of power.

The first time I hit someone, it wasn't because I wanted to hurt them. It was because I didn't know how else to protect myself. I had seen my mother beat me and my siblings for as long as I could remember. She didn't need a reason; her fists and whatever object was close at hand were her way of communicating. I grew up in a house where pain was a language, and it was the only one I learned to speak fluently.

I was about five years old when I discovered that I, too, could hurt people. It wasn't something I planned, but it happened. My older sister, the one who seemed to get all the love I craved, had come over for a visit. She was beautiful—clean, dressed in nice clothes, with soft hair that smelled like flowers. Everything about her was everything I wasn't, and I hated her for it.

She didn't mean to make me feel less than. She was kind to me, even when our mother wasn't. But kindness didn't feel good to me. It felt like a reminder of everything I didn't have, of everything I could never be. I was a dirty, neglected child, always bruised and battered, covered in the filth of our roach-infested house. My sister, on the other hand, was what I imagined girls were supposed to be—lovely, cherished, and perfect. And for that, I resented her.

That night, when she went to bed, I sat awake, stewing in my anger. The voice in my head told me that she didn't deserve what she had. She didn't deserve to be beautiful and loved while I was left to rot. I had been hurt so many times, and I wanted her to feel it, too. I wanted her to know what it was like to be me, to be the one who suffered in silence.

So, I crept into her room. I didn't even think about what I was doing; my body just moved, driven by the rage bubbling inside me. I climbed into bed with her and, without a word, touched her the way I had been touched by so many others. I didn't understand it then, but I wasn't just hurting her—I was trying to communicate with her, to make her understand my pain the only way I knew how.

She didn't fight back. She didn't scream. She just lay there, confused and silent, as I violated her in the same way I had been violated. In my child's mind, I thought that if I could make her feel what I felt, maybe we could share the burden. Maybe I wouldn't be so alone in my misery.

But when it was over, I didn't feel better. I didn't feel powerful or in control. I felt empty. I had become the very thing I despised, and I didn't know how to stop it. The seeds of violence had sprouted, and I was powerless to pull them out.

As I grew older, that violence became a more regular part of my life. It wasn't just about the physical abuse I endured—it was about how I learned to use violence to protect myself, to get what I wanted, to survive. If someone looked at me the wrong way, I would lash out. If someone said something that made me feel small, I would make sure they knew I wasn't to be messed with.

In school, I became known as the girl you didn't want to cross. I didn't care about making friends or being liked. I cared about making sure no one could ever hurt me again. If that meant hurting others first, then so be it. I was quick with my fists, faster with my words, and I developed a reputation for being mean, cruel, and unpredictable.

There was a particular satisfaction in the power I felt when I could make someone flinch or cry with just a look or a sharp insult. It was a way of reclaiming control over a life where I had none. In a world that had taken so much from me, violence became the one thing I could give back. And if I had to hurt others to protect myself, I convinced myself that it was justified.

But as I honed my ability to hurt others, I didn't realize how much I was hurting myself. Every time I lashed out, every time I bullied or manipulated someone, I was feeding the same cycle of violence that had been inflicted on me. I was becoming exactly what I hated, and I didn't know how to stop.

The turning point came when I found myself in relationships where I was the one causing the harm. I didn't want to be vulnerable, so I made sure to dominate and control my partners before they could ever get close enough to hurt me. I would push them away, physically and emotionally, hitting and yelling when I felt threatened. I justified my behavior by telling myself that I was just protecting myself from being hurt again. But in reality, I was perpetuating the same abuse I had grown up with.

When I was married, I carried that same violence into my relationship. My ex-husband was a kind man, someone who genuinely wanted to love and take care of me. But I didn't know how to accept that kind of love. It scared me. So, I would shove him, force him to do things he didn't want to do, and beat on him when I couldn't control my own rage. I thought that if he stayed, it meant he loved me. If he let me hurt him, it meant I was in control.

But one day, he didn't stay. He left me, just like I had always feared. And in that moment, I realized that all the violence, all the cruelty—it had done nothing but drive away the very thing I wanted most: love.

The seeds of violence that had been planted in me as a child had grown into a full-blown forest of destruction. I had become the offender, the one who hurt others, the one who pushed people away. I had molested my sister, beaten my husband, and destroyed any chance I had at a normal, loving relationship.

But as I stood in the wreckage of my life, I knew something had to change. I couldn't keep living this way, hurting others and myself in the process. The seeds of violence had taken root, but I wasn't sure how to dig them out.

The road to healing would be long, and it would take more than just stopping the violent behaviors. I would have to confront the pain, the trauma, and the deep-rooted anger that had driven me for so long. I would have to face the truth of what I had become and, somehow, find a way to become something else.

For now, though, all I knew was that I had to try. Because if I didn't, the violence would consume me completely. And I wasn't ready to let that happen. Not yet.

Chapter 4: Nefarious Self-Sabotage

Adulthood didn't offer me any escape from the pain of my past—it only sharpened it. The violence I had embraced as a child grew more sophisticated as I got older, taking on new forms as I spiraled further into self-destruction. The seeds of violence that had taken root in my soul continued to grow, morphing into behaviors that I knew were sabotaging my life, yet I couldn't seem to stop myself. In my darkest moments, I found a strange kind of comfort in my suffering, as if the chaos was the only thing that felt familiar, even safe.

Every relationship I entered was doomed before it even began. I didn't know how to be in a healthy relationship. How could I? The only love I'd ever known was twisted, violent, and conditional. I believed that pain was a necessary part of love, that intimacy came with a price—a price I was all too willing to pay, even if it meant tearing myself apart in the process.

I found myself drawn to men who mirrored the worst parts of me. They were broken, just like I was, but their brokenness only fueled my own self-sabotage. I chose partners who would hurt me, who would reinforce the narrative I had been taught my whole life: that I wasn't worth anything, that I deserved to be mistreated, that violence was the only language I truly understood.

When things would start to go well—when a man would show me real care, real kindness—I would panic. The thought of being loved without conditions terrified me. It made me feel vulnerable, exposed. So, I would do what I always did: I would destroy it. I would pick fights, push them away, accuse them of things they hadn't done, and hurt them before they had a chance to hurt me. It was always the same pattern. I couldn't let anyone get close enough to see the real me because I believed that if they did, they would leave me anyway.

But even as I clung to this violent persona, the one who lashed out and caused pain, I began to notice something else stirring inside me—something that scared me even more than the violence. Beneath the layers of anger, shame, and self-loathing, there was a small, fragile voice whispering that maybe, just maybe, I was worth more than this. That maybe I didn't have to live like this forever.

These glimmers of my own strength were fleeting, like small cracks in the armor I had built around myself. When they appeared, I would quickly shove them back down, convincing myself that they were lies, that I wasn't capable of anything more than the destruction I had been born into. But deep down, I knew that wasn't true. Deep down, I knew I had survived things that should have broken me, and yet, here I was—still standing. There had to be a reason for that. There had to be something more than just surviving.

But the pull of self-sabotage was strong. It was like I had been programmed to fail, to ruin any chance of happiness before it even had a chance to take root. I would start to see a glimmer of hope—a job opportunity, a relationship that felt healthy, a moment of peace—and I would ruin it. I would miss deadlines, show up late, pick fights, or engage in behaviors that I knew would lead to failure. It was as if I couldn't allow myself to succeed. Success felt foreign, dangerous even. The only thing I knew how to handle was failure, and so I clung to it like a security blanket.

There was a part of me that believed I didn't deserve to be happy. That I was too broken, too damaged to ever experience real joy. So, I would sabotage anything that looked like it could lead to something good. I would push people away, quit jobs, and engage in reckless behavior, convincing myself that this was just who I was—someone who couldn't be saved.

The worst part was, I knew what I was doing. I could see it happening, like watching a car crash in slow motion, but I couldn't stop it. Every time I hurt someone I loved, every time I destroyed something good in my life, I would tell myself it was better this way. It was better to be the one causing the pain than the one feeling it.

But deep down, the cracks were starting to spread. The violent persona I had built for myself was no longer impenetrable. I could feel the weight of it, crushing me from the inside out. I was tired—tired of the violence, tired of the self-sabotage, tired of feeling like I was trapped in a life that wasn't mine. I wanted to believe that there was something more for me, but I didn't know how to get there. I didn't know how to break free from the cycle of destruction I had been trapped in for so long.

And so, I continued to spiral, clinging to the only identity I had ever known—the "violent" girl, the one who hurt others before they could hurt her, the one who destroyed any chance of happiness before it could destroy her. But even as I clung to that identity, I could feel it slipping away. The seeds of violence had grown into a tangled mess, but I wasn't sure I wanted to live in that mess anymore.

There was a small part of me—a part I was terrified to acknowledge—that believed I could be something more. That maybe, just maybe, I could stop sabotaging myself. But that part of me was buried so deep under the weight of my past that I wasn't sure I could ever find it.

For now, though, I was stuck in the spiral, clinging to the violence that had defined me for so long. But deep down, I knew that something had to give. I couldn't keep living this way. I couldn't keep sabotaging myself, destroying everything good in my life just to prove that I was unworthy of happiness. Something had to change.

But change, I knew, wouldn't come easy. And I wasn't sure I was ready for it yet.

Chapter 5: Neglectful and Needy

My early adulthood was like being lost in a maze where every turn led back to the same dark corner. I was trying to escape the storm of my past, but no matter where I ran, I kept ending up right back in the middle of it. I had learned early on that my needs didn't matter—at least not to the people who should have cared for me. I had grown so used to neglect that I didn't even recognize it when I neglected myself. I didn't know how to nurture or care for my own emotional needs because, deep down, I didn't believe I deserved it.

I started to realize that I had a void inside me—an emptiness I couldn't ignore. It was like a bottomless pit, constantly begging to be filled, but no matter what I tried to stuff into it, nothing worked. I didn't know how to fill that void in healthy ways. So, I turned to the only things I knew: destructive relationships and self-sabotage. I was desperate for someone—anyone—to tell me I was worth something. I thought if I could just find the right person, they would fix me, make me whole. But instead, I found people who were just as broken as I was, and all they did was make the void bigger.

I threw myself into relationships with men who mirrored the pain I carried inside. They were needy, possessive, and full of their own insecurities. But instead of seeing them for what they were—warning signs—I saw them as validation.

Their attention, no matter how toxic, made me feel like I mattered. It was like an addiction: the more they needed me, the more I felt like I had a purpose. But it wasn't real. It wasn't love. It was two broken people trying to use each other to fill the cracks in their own souls.

There was one man, in particular, who stood out during this time. His name was Marcus, and from the moment we met, I could sense the darkness in him. He was charming at first, saying all the right things to make me feel seen. He told me I was beautiful, that I was special, that I was everything he had ever wanted. But it didn't take long for the cracks in his charm to show. He was possessive, constantly accusing me of things I hadn't done, just like my grandfather used to. But instead of running from the red flags, I leaned into them. I thought if Marcus needed me that much, maybe I could fix him. Maybe, in fixing him, I could fix myself.

But it didn't take long for Marcus to become controlling. He would demand to know where I was at all times, who I was talking to, and what I was doing. If I didn't answer his calls right away, he would accuse me of cheating, of lying, of being worthless. And every time he said those things, something inside me believed him. I believed I was worthless. I believed I was the problem. But I also believed that I could fix it. If I just tried harder, if I just loved him enough, maybe I could make him see that I was good enough.

It wasn't just Marcus. There were others, too. Men who treated me like I was disposable. They would use me, take what they wanted, and then leave. And every time they left, the void inside me grew bigger. But instead of walking away from these men, I would chase them, desperate for their approval, desperate for someone to fill the emptiness I felt. I clung to them like they were my lifeline, even though I knew they were dragging me deeper into the darkness.

The more I neglected my own needs, the needier I became for their attention. I would do anything to keep them around, even if it meant sacrificing my dignity, my self-respect, and my emotional well-being. I allowed them to treat me like I was nothing because, deep down, that's what I believed I was. Nothing. I had convinced myself that this was all I deserved. That this was what love looked like for someone like me.

The worst part was, I knew I was stuck. I could feel it in every relationship, in every desperate attempt to fill the void with people who only made me feel worse about myself. But I didn't know how to change. I didn't know how to break free from the cycle of neglect and neediness. I didn't even know where to start. I thought that maybe if I just found the right person, someone who could see past all my brokenness, they would save me. But no one came. And the more I tried to fill the void with these toxic relationships, the more I realized that no one could save me but myself.

I wasn't ready to face that truth, though. Not yet. So, I kept running from it, bouncing from one unhealthy relationship to the next, hoping that somehow, things would change. But they never did. They couldn't. Not until I was willing to face the real issue: that the void inside me couldn't be filled by someone else. It had to be filled by me. And that was the scariest thought of all because I had no idea how to even begin doing that.

But somewhere, deep inside, I knew I couldn't keep living this way. I knew that if I didn't find a way to change, I would destroy myself. And that was the one thing I wasn't willing to do. Not yet. I had survived too much to let my own self-destruction be the thing that finally took me down. But knowing I needed to change and actually knowing how to change were two very different things. And I was still stuck in the middle of that dark, endless maze, trying to find my way out.

The truth was, I had never learned how to love myself. I didn't even know where to start. But if I was ever going to break free from the cycle of neglect and neediness, I had to figure it out. And that realization, terrifying as it was, was the first step toward something I wasn't sure I deserved: healing.

For now, though, I was still lost. Still clinging to the hope that someone, anyone, would come along and show me the way out. Still neglecting my own needs, still desperately seeking validation from people who would never be able to give it to me. But deep down, the cracks were starting to form. And even though I didn't know it yet, those cracks would eventually lead to something I had never thought possible: my own transformation.

Chapter 6: Narcissistic Rage

The rage came in waves, like a storm building on the horizon, each gust more forceful than the last. At first, it was just a simmer, an irritation I couldn't quite shake, but soon enough, it boiled over. I could feel it before it even reached my lips—the tightening in my chest, the burning heat in my veins. It was a familiar feeling, one I had known since childhood, one that had saved me, protected me, when there was nothing else to hold on to.

But now, in adulthood, it was destroying me.

I would lose myself in those moments of rage, a tidal wave of anger crashing down over everything I had tried so hard to hold together. I had spent years building walls, keeping my emotions at bay, numbing myself to the pain. But when the rage came, those walls shattered. I would scream, lash out, break things. It didn't matter who was in the way—anyone near me became a target. And I didn't care. In those moments, I felt powerful, invincible. My voice filled the room, my fists slammed into anything within reach. The world had to feel what I felt, had to understand the chaos inside me.

The worst part was, I knew where it came from. Every time I let the rage take over, I saw flashes of the past—my grandfather's face, his hands, his fists, his voice calling me worthless. I would hear the echoes of those nights when he stood over me, angry at something I didn't understand, using his strength to dominate, to punish, to control. His betrayal had left a scar so deep that even as an adult, I couldn't shake the feeling that I had to fight for my life every time someone pushed me too far.

It wasn't just him, though. My mother's madness, the way she would scream and beat me, her naked body a constant reminder of her own brokenness, had imprinted on me. I had learned from her that rage was the only way to survive. When you were vulnerable, you were weak. When you were weak, you were hurt. So I had made myself hard, violent, impenetrable. But now, it was turning me into the very thing I had spent my life fighting against.

There were moments where I'd see it—glimpses of who I had become, and it terrified me.

One night, during one of my worst breakdowns, I found myself standing in the middle of my kitchen, surrounded by broken dishes and shattered glass. I had thrown a plate against the wall so hard that it exploded into pieces, shards raining down like confetti. My hands shook, my breath coming in ragged gasps as I tried to catch up to what had just happened. My daughter, barely four years old, stood frozen in the doorway, her eyes wide with fear.

"Mommy, please stop," she whispered, her voice trembling.

Her words hit me like a freight train, cutting through the rage like a knife. I had seen that look before—the wide eyes, the trembling lip, the sheer terror on her face. It was the same look I used to have when my grandfather would come into my room at night, the same look I saw on my reflection when my mother would hit me.

And suddenly, it wasn't just my rage I was seeing—it was his. My grandfather's face flashed in my mind, his voice accusing me of things I hadn't done, calling me ugly, stupid, worthless. His fists, slamming into my small body, his hands ripping away at what little innocence I had left. I saw my mother's vacant eyes as she swung whatever she could find at me, her anger wild and unpredictable.

And now, here I was, doing the same thing to my own child.

I sank to my knees in front of her, my breath catching in my throat. I couldn't stop shaking. The rage had turned into something else—something I couldn't even name. I looked up at her, at the tears streaming down her face, and I knew, in that moment, that I had become the very thing I had sworn I would never be.

"I'm sorry," I whispered, my voice breaking.

But what good were apologies? What could I possibly say to undo the fear I had put into her eyes? I had become the monster in her life, just like my abusers had been in mine. And that realization shattered me more than any rage ever could.

For days after that, I couldn't look at her without feeling the weight of my own failures. I had promised myself, after everything I had been through, that I would never pass the pain onto her. But I had. And the worst part was, I didn't even know how to stop it.

The more I thought about it, the more I realized that my rage wasn't just about the people in front of me—it was about the people behind me. My grandfather, my mother, the men who had taken advantage of me, the world that had treated me like nothing more than a disposable object. I was still fighting them, even though they weren't in the room anymore. I was still trying to defend myself against ghosts.

But the real question was, who was going to save me from myself?

The anger, the violence, the narcissistic need to control everything around me—it was all I had left. It was the only thing that had kept me alive. But now, it was threatening to take everything I loved away from me. I was trapped in a cycle of destruction, and I didn't know how to break free.

One night, after my daughter had fallen asleep, I sat alone in the dark, staring at the ceiling. The house was quiet, but my mind was racing. I couldn't stop thinking about how my rage had nearly ruined everything. I thought about all the times I had lashed out at people who didn't deserve it—my friends, my family, my child. I thought about all the broken relationships, the hurtful words, the violence that had become so normal to me.

And in that quiet, something shifted. A small, fragile thought crept into my mind, something I hadn't allowed myself to consider before: Maybe I didn't have to be this way. Maybe I could stop fighting. Maybe I could let go of the rage.

But letting go meant being vulnerable. And being vulnerable meant risking everything. Could I really afford that?

I closed my eyes, feeling the weight of the years pressing down on me. For the first time in a long time, I prayed—not for strength, but for the courage to stop fighting. To stop being violent. To stop letting the rage control me.

I didn't know how to change. I didn't know if I even could. But for the first time, I was willing to try. And maybe, just maybe, that was enough to start.

Chapter 7: The Voice of God

The night was thick with silence, a suffocating kind of quiet that pressed down on Violet like the weight of her past. She lay awake in the darkness, her body exhausted, her mind racing. Sleep had become a distant memory, replaced by a restless energy that gnawed at her insides. Her daughter was sleeping soundly in the next room, but Violet couldn't find peace. Not after what had happened. Not after seeing the fear in her daughter's eyes.

She replayed the scene over and over in her mind—her own hands shaking with rage, the shattered glass, her daughter's trembling voice begging her to stop. The memory cut deeper than any wound she had ever known. It was a mirror, showing her the reflection of someone she didn't recognize, someone she had vowed never to become.

Violent. Angry. Unforgiving.

She had spent her whole life fighting—fighting to survive, fighting to be seen, fighting to escape the horrors of her childhood. But now, the fight had turned inward. She was battling herself, and she was losing.

That night, as Violet lay in the stillness, something shifted. It was subtle at first, like the faintest breeze stirring the air. But then it grew, a presence that filled the room, pressing into the darkest corners of her mind. It wasn't something she could see, but she could feel it—something powerful, something… divine.

In that silence, a voice broke through. It wasn't loud or forceful. In fact, it was gentle, like a whisper carried on the wind. But it cut through the noise in her head, and it spoke directly to her heart.

"You don't have to be violent."

The words stopped her cold. She sat up, her heart pounding, her breath caught in her throat. Had she imagined it? Was it just her mind playing tricks on her? But the voice came again, soft and unwavering.

"You don't have to carry the 'N.' You can let it go."

Tears welled in Violet's eyes, spilling over before she could stop them. She had been called so many things in her life—ugly, stupid, floozy, violent—but no one had ever told her she didn't have to carry it. No one had ever given her permission to let it go.

"Who am I without it?" she whispered into the darkness.

For so long, she had believed that the violence was part of her. It was her shield, her defense, her way of surviving in a world that had shown her nothing but cruelty. Without it, who would she be? How would she protect herself? How would she keep the world from crushing her again?

But the voice, steady and kind, spoke again. "You are not your past. You are not what they called you. You can be something new."

The words hit her like a flood, washing over her, filling every empty space inside her that had been hollowed out by pain. For the first time in her life, Violet felt something other than anger. She felt... hope.

Could it be true? Could she really let go of the names, the labels, the violence that had defined her for so long? Could she really be something else—someone else?

She wiped her tears with trembling hands, her mind swirling with questions. She thought of the years she had spent trapped in her own rage, of the countless times she had lashed out, hurt people, and pushed them away. She had always justified it, telling herself that it was the only way to survive, the only way to keep the world from devouring her whole.

But now, in this quiet, sacred moment, she realized something she had never allowed herself to believe before: survival wasn't the same as living.

For so long, she had been surviving, just barely holding on, but she had never truly lived. Not freely. Not without the weight of her past crushing her every step. She had carried the "N"—the narcissism, the negativity, the numbing rage—like a badge, like armor. But that armor had turned into chains, and those chains had kept her from becoming who she was meant to be.

"Violet," she whispered to herself, testing the name on her lips. Could she really be Violet? Could she really be something beautiful, something strong, something soft?

She closed her eyes, and for the first time in as long as she could remember, she prayed. It wasn't a formal prayer, not the kind she had heard in church, but a raw, desperate plea. She prayed for strength, for forgiveness, for the courage to let go of the "N" that had defined her for so long.

"God," she whispered, her voice cracking. "If you're really there, if you can hear me... I need you. I don't want to be violent anymore. I don't want to carry this pain. Please, help me."

The silence that followed was different this time. It wasn't heavy or suffocating. It was peaceful, almost comforting. And in that peace, she felt it—God's presence, wrapping around her like a warm embrace.

"You don't have to be violent anymore," the voice whispered again, but this time, it wasn't just a voice in her head. It was the voice of God, speaking to her soul, offering her a way out, offering her a chance to be free.

She didn't know how to do it. She didn't know where to start. But for the first time, Violet believed that change was possible. She believed that she could be more than what had happened to her. She could be more than the violence, more than the pain.

She could be Violet.

And with that belief came a flicker of hope, small but steady, like a single flame in the dark. It wasn't much, but it was enough. Enough to make her want to try. Enough to make her want to fight—not against the world, but for herself.

As she lay back down, tears still wet on her cheeks, she felt something shift deep inside her. The storm that had raged for so long was still there, but it had quieted, just enough for her to hear the whisper of hope.

"You are not the 'N,' Violet. You never were. You are something more. You are something beautiful."

And for the first time in a long time, Violet believed it.

Chapter 8: Removing the 'N'

The morning after hearing God's voice, Violet woke with a feeling she hadn't experienced in years—lightness. It wasn't that her problems had disappeared or that the pain had been erased overnight. Far from it. But there was something different, something small yet powerful, a whisper of hope that had taken root in her heart. She clung to it like a lifeline, determined not to let go, even as the storm of her past loomed on the horizon.

As she sat at the small kitchen table, staring into the mug of coffee she hadn't touched, her mind raced. She could still feel the weight of the "N" traits clinging to her—Negativity, Numbing, Narcissism, Nefariousness—but now, for the first time, she could see them clearly for what they were: chains. They had kept her bound to the pain, to the anger, to the violence. They had been her armor, but they had also been her prison.

"How do I remove them?" she whispered to herself, the question hanging in the air like a challenge. Where do I even begin?

Negativity, she thought. That's where I'll start. If she could just stop seeing the world through a lens of despair, maybe—just maybe—she could begin to change. But it wasn't as simple as flipping a switch. The Negativity had been with her for so long that it felt like a part of her identity. She was the girl who expected the worst, who saw every glass as half-empty, every opportunity as a trap. It was how she had survived.

But survival wasn't enough anymore.

She took a deep breath and made a decision. If she was going to do this—if she was really going to change—she couldn't do it alone.

Later that afternoon, Violet found herself walking down a narrow street toward a small brick church on the corner. She had passed it countless times before, never giving it a second thought. But today, something had drawn her there. It wasn't Sunday, so the church was mostly empty, but she could hear faint voices coming from one of the rooms. The sound of quiet conversation and occasional laughter echoed through the halls.

She hesitated at the door, unsure of what she was even doing there. She didn't belong in a place like this—did she? Her life had been full of too much darkness, too much violence. What would they think of her? What could she possibly say to make them understand?

But as she stood there, wrestling with her doubts, the door opened, and an older woman stepped out, nearly bumping into her.

"Oh, I'm so sorry!" the woman exclaimed with a warm smile. "I didn't see you there."

Violet stepped back, mumbling an apology, ready to turn and walk away, but the woman reached out and touched her arm gently.

"Are you okay, dear?" the woman asked, her eyes kind and concerned.

Something in the woman's voice, in her gentle touch, made Violet stop. She wasn't okay. She hadn't been okay in a very long time. And suddenly, standing there on the steps of the church, all the walls she had built around herself began to crumble.

"I—I don't know," Violet stammered. "I'm just... I need help."

The woman's smile softened, and she nodded as if she understood. "Come inside. Let's talk."

Inside the small church office, the woman introduced herself as Pastor Marie. Her presence was calming, and there was a strength about her that made Violet feel safe, like she didn't need to hide anymore.

For a while, Violet sat in silence, unsure of where to start. But Pastor Marie waited patiently, giving her the space she needed.

"I've been hearing this voice," Violet finally said, her words slow and measured. "It told me I don't have to be violent anymore. That I can be… different."

Pastor Marie nodded, her eyes full of understanding. "That voice," she said softly, "sounds a lot like God."

Violet let the words sink in. "But I don't know how to be different," she admitted. "I've been this way for so long. Angry. Bitter. Negative. I don't even know where to start."

Pastor Marie leaned forward slightly, her hands folded on the desk. "The fact that you want to start is already a step in the right direction, Violet. None of us change overnight. It's a journey—sometimes a long one—but it begins with one step. And you've already taken it by being here."

"I've been carrying these things with me for so long," Violet continued. "All this… negativity. I expect the worst from people. I expect the worst from myself. It's like I'm stuck in this cycle, and I can't get out."

Pastor Marie smiled gently. "You're not alone, Violet. Many of us carry heavy burdens from our past. But God didn't create you to be stuck in that cycle. He created you for something more."

"But how do I change?" Violet asked, her voice small, almost childlike. "How do I stop being… this?"

"It starts with recognizing the lies you've believed about yourself," Pastor Marie said. "That you're not good enough, that you're unworthy of love, that you're destined to fail. Those are the lies that feed your negativity. But those lies aren't from God. He sees you differently. He sees the real you—the Violet underneath all the hurt."

Violet swallowed hard, the tears prickling at the corners of her eyes again. Could it really be true? Could she really be more than the labels she had carried all her life?

Pastor Marie leaned back in her chair, her expression thoughtful. "I think God's been working in your heart for a while now, Violet. You're already starting to see things differently, and that's the first step. But it's not easy. Removing these 'N' traits—like negativity, narcissism, numbing—they don't disappear overnight. It takes work, faith, and a willingness to confront the darkest parts of yourself."

Violet nodded slowly, her heart heavy but hopeful. "I want to change," she said quietly. "I want to let go of the negativity, but it's so hard. Every time I try, it's like I fall back into the same patterns."

Pastor Marie reached across the table and took Violet's hands in her own. "You don't have to do it alone. God will walk with you every step of the way. And I'll be here too. We'll work on it together, one step at a time."

For the first time in what felt like forever, Violet smiled—just a small, tentative smile—but it was real. There was a long road ahead of her, but for the first time, she believed it was a road she could walk. And she wouldn't be walking it alone.

That evening, as Violet lay in bed, she thought about what Pastor Marie had said. The lies she had believed about herself—the lies that had fed her negativity—had started to lose their power. The words that had once defined her—ugly, stupid, floozy—were starting to fade. In their place, something new was beginning to grow.

As she drifted off to sleep, she whispered a quiet prayer, thanking God for the first step and for the strength to take another one tomorrow.

The journey to remove the "N" had begun.

Chapter 9: Confronting the Past

Violet sat at the edge of her bed, the old journal lying open in her lap. Its pages were filled with the scribbled memories she had long tried to bury—fragments of a past she had spent years running from. The memories were sharp, jagged things that threatened to cut her every time she tried to pick them up. But if she was going to heal, if she was truly going to remove the "N" and step into her new identity, she knew she had to face them.

She glanced at the blank sheet of paper on the nightstand next to her. Writing the letter had been Pastor Marie's idea—a way to release the poison that had built up inside her over the years. At first, the thought of confronting her past through words seemed absurd. How could writing to people who had hurt her—people who had broken her in ways that still felt irreparable—do anything but reopen wounds?

But deep down, Violet knew this was part of her journey. She couldn't move forward until she stopped hiding from the shadows of her past.

Her hands shook as she picked up the pen, and for a long moment, she just stared at the page, unsure where to begin. The faces of the people who had shaped her pain flashed before her—her mother, her stepbrother, her grandfather. The weight of those memories pressed down on her chest, making it hard to breathe.

Finally, she pressed the pen to the paper and began to write.

Dear Mom,

I don't know how to start this letter. There's so much I want to say, but at the same time, I'm afraid to say it. I'm afraid that once I start, the floodgates will open, and I'll never be able to stop. But I have to try, because I can't keep living like this—carrying this weight inside me.

For so long, I hated you. I hated you for the things you did, for the way you treated me and my siblings. I hated you for the times you chose men over us, for the times you let them hurt me, for the times you hurt me yourself. I hated you for being broken, for being sick, for being someone I couldn't rely on.

But now, as I sit here, I realize that my hatred has only kept me trapped. It hasn't hurt you—it's only hurt me. And if I'm going to move forward, I have to let it go. I have to stop letting the past control me.

I forgive you, Mom.

I know that doesn't erase what happened. It doesn't make the pain go away, and it doesn't mean I forget. But I forgive you, not for you, but for me. I forgive you because I need to be free.

I hope that wherever you are now, you've found peace. I hope that you know I don't hate you anymore. I hope that somehow, you're proud of the woman I'm becoming, even though I'm still finding my way.

Love,
Violet

The tears fell freely as Violet finished the letter, but this time, they weren't tears of anger or resentment. They were tears of release, of relief. The weight she had carried for so long—the hatred, the blame, the guilt—it wasn't gone, but it had started to lift, just a little. And that was enough.

Next, she turned her thoughts to her grandfather, her hand hovering over the paper as memories of him flooded her mind. The abuse. The betrayal. The way he had twisted her life into something unrecognizable. This letter was harder—so much harder. But she knew it was necessary.

Dear Grandfather,

There are no words for what you did to me. No words that can capture the way you stole my childhood, my innocence, my sense of self. You were supposed to protect me, to love me. Instead, you destroyed me.

For years, I've carried the weight of what you did. I've carried it like a stone around my neck, dragging me down into the darkest places. I've hated you with every fiber of my being, and I've let that hatred shape me—turn me into someone I never wanted to be. I became violent, angry, and full of rage. I hurt others the way you hurt me because I didn't know any other way to live.

But today, I'm choosing something different.

I'm choosing to forgive you.

Not because you deserve it. God knows you don't. But because I deserve to be free. I deserve to live without the shadow of what you did hanging over me. I deserve peace.

So I forgive you. I forgive you so that I can let go of the hatred that has poisoned me for so long. I forgive you because I refuse to let you have any more power over my life.

I don't know if I'll ever understand why you did what you did, and I'm not sure it matters anymore. What matters is that I'm taking back control. I'm reclaiming my life.

I hope that one day, I can truly let go of the pain you caused. I hope that one day, the memory of you won't hurt so much. But for now, I'll take this first step.

Violet

When she finished, Violet set the pen down and closed her eyes, her chest rising and falling with each deep breath. The letters weren't perfect. They didn't fix everything. But they were a start.

For so long, Violet had been running from her past—burying it, denying it, pretending it didn't exist. But now, for the first time, she had faced it head-on. She had confronted the people who had hurt her, and in doing so, she had started the process of healing.

It wasn't over. The journey was far from complete. But as Violet sat there, wiping the last of her tears, she realized that she didn't feel quite as heavy as before. The chains of the past had loosened just a little.

In the weeks that followed, Violet continued to confront her past—through therapy, through prayer, through more letters she would never send. She faced the memories that had haunted her for so long, peeling back the layers of hurt, anger, and shame one by one. It wasn't easy. In fact, it was the hardest thing she had ever done. But each time she confronted a piece of her past, she felt a little lighter, a little freer.

One day, while sitting in Pastor Marie's office, Violet spoke words she never thought she would say.

"I forgive myself."

The pastor looked at her with soft eyes, nodding in approval. "And how does that feel?"

Violet smiled, a small but genuine smile. "It feels like I can breathe again."

In that moment, Violet realized that forgiveness wasn't just about letting go of the past. It was about giving herself permission to move forward. To live without the weight of shame and guilt. To embrace the woman she was becoming.

She was no longer Ugly, Stupid, or Floozy. She was Violet—full of grace, strength, and light. And for the first time, she was starting to believe it.

Chapter 10: Narcissistic to Nurturing

For the first time in her life, Violet felt something unfamiliar: peace. It wasn't a grand or dramatic shift, but it was there, like a soft light glowing in a room that had once been filled with shadows. It had taken her years to understand the concept of nurturing—an idea that had felt foreign for so long, especially after living a life built on survival, violence, and self-sabotage.

Growing up, Violet had believed that to survive, she had to become the center of her own world. She had learned to manipulate, to control, to wield the little power she had over others just to feel some semblance of safety. That had been her armor—the only way she knew how to protect herself from a world that had always been against her.

But now, as she sat quietly in her tiny apartment, sipping tea and reading a passage from her Bible, she felt something different stir inside her. Instead of seeking power over others, she was beginning to seek peace within herself. The once overwhelming need to be seen, to be heard, to dominate her relationships had begun to melt away, making space for something gentler.

It hadn't happened overnight. In fact, learning to nurture herself was the most difficult thing Violet had ever faced. Her whole life had been built on the belief that she didn't deserve love, that she wasn't worthy of kindness or tenderness. But as she worked through her past, with each "N" trait she removed, she was slowly realizing that she was worthy—worthy of love, worthy of care, and worthy of peace.

Sitting in her favorite chair, she glanced at the photo on the wall—a picture of her daughter. It had been years since Violet had seen her, but their relationship was slowly being repaired. Her daughter had been distant for so long, hurt by the same rage and narcissism that had once ruled Violet's life. But after months of letters, phone calls, and gentle outreach, Violet felt the first signs of a bond forming again.

It was a start.

Her phone buzzed, breaking her thoughts. She picked it up and saw a message from Carla, a woman she had recently met at church. They had connected over a Bible study group, and for the first time in a long time, Violet had felt comfortable making a friend. In the past, she had used relationships to fill her own voids—pulling people close only to manipulate or control them. But this time, she was trying something different. She was trying to let the relationship grow naturally, with no strings attached, no expectations other than kindness.

The message was simple: "Hey, Violet, would you like to grab lunch tomorrow? I'd love to chat."

Smiling, Violet typed back, "I'd love to. How about noon?"

After sending the message, she set the phone down and leaned back in her chair. Making friends, nurturing relationships—it all felt so new. But in this season of her life, she was determined to be different. She was learning, little by little, how to show love without taking from others. How to give without expecting something in return.

Her journey wasn't perfect. There were still moments when the old patterns threatened to resurface—moments when she wanted to pull people closer for the wrong reasons, to control them as a way to keep herself safe. But she was learning to catch herself before those impulses took over. She was learning to pause, to breathe, and to ask herself: How can I show love here? How can I nurture instead of control?

One of the greatest lessons she had learned was how to nurture herself. For years, Violet had neglected her own needs, masking her pain with destructive behaviors. But now, she was learning to care for herself in a way she never had before. She took time each day to pray, to meditate, to write in her journal. She was finding peace in the small moments—like tending to the tiny plants she had placed by her windowsill, watering them with care, watching them grow. Each little sprout was a reminder of her own growth, of how far she had come.

Violet had also begun to nurture her relationship with God. The voice she had heard in her darkest moments—the one that told her she didn't have to carry the "N" anymore—had become her lifeline. In the quiet of her mornings, she would sit with her Bible open, praying for guidance, for strength, and for the grace to continue her transformation.

One passage in particular had become her mantra: "And the peace of God, which transcends all understanding, will guard your hearts and your minds in Christ Jesus." (Philippians 4:7)

She had written it on a piece of paper and taped it to her bathroom mirror, repeating it to herself every morning as she brushed her teeth, as she prepared for the day. The peace of God was now what she sought—not the chaos of control, not the fleeting comfort of manipulation, but the true, lasting peace that came from surrendering her life to a higher purpose.

That evening, Violet met with Pastor Marie for their regular one-on-one session. Pastor Marie had been a steady guide throughout Violet's transformation, offering wisdom and support as Violet worked to remove each "N" trait.

"I'm starting to feel lighter," Violet said, sipping her tea as they sat across from each other. "I'm not perfect, but I'm learning to love without needing to control. I'm learning to be kind—to myself and to others."

Pastor Marie smiled, her eyes full of warmth. "That's the beauty of nurturing, Violet. When we nurture ourselves, we create the space to nurture others. And love—real, true love—can only grow in that kind of space."

Violet nodded. "I've spent so much of my life trying to fill the emptiness inside me by controlling people, by making them give me what I thought I needed. But now, I'm starting to see that love doesn't come from taking—it comes from giving. And that starts with giving to myself first."

Pastor Marie reached across the table and gently placed her hand on Violet's. "You've come a long way, my dear. And the more you continue to nurture yourself, the more you'll see God's love flourish in your life."

Violet felt a sense of peace wash over her. For the first time, she believed those words. She was learning to nurture herself and others, letting go of the toxic patterns that had once defined her. She was beginning to understand that true power didn't come from control—it came from love.

As she left the church that night, walking under the soft glow of the streetlights, Violet knew that she was no longer the violent girl she had once been. The "N" had been removed, and in its place, a new Violet had bloomed—one who was capable of nurturing, of loving, and of living in peace.

And for the first time in her life, she felt truly free.

Chapter 11: Numbing to Feeling

For years, Violet had become a master at pushing down her emotions, burying them so deep inside herself that even she couldn't find them. The numbness had been her shield, her way of surviving the unbearable weight of her trauma. But now, in this moment, as she sat in the quiet of her apartment, something was shifting.

The numbness was cracking.

It started slowly at first, like a hairline fracture in glass. Small moments would bring it out—a kind word from a stranger, a hymn at church that touched a chord in her heart, a memory from her childhood that surfaced unexpectedly. But now, sitting in the stillness, it wasn't just a crack anymore. The numbness was shattering.

Violet had spent years building walls, layering her heart with bricks of anger, resentment, and shame to keep the pain out. But with those walls crumbling, she could feel everything—every ache, every sorrow, every wound she had ignored for so long.

And it terrified her.

She had always feared that if she let herself feel, really feel, she would be consumed by the emotions. She believed the grief would be too much, the pain too overwhelming. But as she sat there, tears streaming down her face, she realized something she had never understood before: feeling wasn't a sign of weakness. It was a sign of being alive.

Her chest heaved as the sobs racked her body, shaking her to her core. It wasn't just sadness—it was a flood of emotions she had locked away for decades. She was grieving for the little girl she had once been, the one who had been called ugly, stupid, and floozy. She was mourning the innocence that had been stolen from her, the childhood that had been torn apart by violence and abuse.

The memories came rushing back, and for the first time, she didn't push them away. She allowed herself to remember—to remember the smell of her grandfather's cologne as he hurt her, to remember the sting of her mother's words, to remember the confusion and fear that had plagued her every day. And she let herself cry for all the moments she had never been allowed to cry before.

The numbness was gone, and in its place was a tidal wave of feeling. It hurt, but it also felt strangely freeing. The more she cried, the more she felt a weight lifting off her shoulders, as if the years of holding it all in were finally being released.

Violet wasn't just crying for herself. She was crying for the people she had hurt, for the relationships she had sabotaged, for the pain she had inflicted on others because she didn't know how to deal with her own. She cried for her daughter, for the lost years when she had been too consumed by her own rage and shame to be the mother her child needed.

As she wiped her tears with the back of her hand, she realized something profound: the feelings she had been running from all these years weren't her enemy. They were her way out. The numbness had protected her for so long, but now, it was feeling that was going to set her free.

It was a few days later when she found herself back in Pastor Marie's office, her hands nervously clasped in her lap. She had come to Pastor Marie for guidance many times, but today felt different. Today, she wasn't seeking advice. She was seeking solace.

"I don't know how to stop crying," Violet said, her voice trembling. "It's like… like once I opened the door, I can't close it. The feelings just keep coming."

Pastor Marie nodded, her expression calm and understanding. "That's because for years, you've been holding it all in, Violet. The numbness was a way to protect yourself, but now you're allowing yourself to heal. And healing requires feeling."

Violet swallowed hard, her throat tight with emotion. "But it's so painful. I don't know how to handle it."

"The pain is real, and it's going to hurt," Pastor Marie said softly. "But you don't have to handle it alone. God is with you in this. He's been with you all along. And He's the one who can help you carry the weight of these feelings."

Violet closed her eyes for a moment, letting the pastor's words wash over her. She had heard it before—God was with her—but somehow, in this moment, it felt different. It felt real. She could feel His presence in her heart, gently guiding her through the storm of emotions.

Over the next few weeks, Violet continued to embrace the power of feeling. It wasn't easy. There were days when the grief would hit her out of nowhere—when a song on the radio or a smell on the street would bring back memories she didn't want to relive. But instead of pushing those feelings away, she let herself experience them.

She cried. She raged. She grieved. And through it all, she began to realize that the feelings weren't as terrifying as she had always believed. In fact, they were healing her. Each tear was like a drop of rain, washing away the years of hurt and shame.

The more she allowed herself to feel, the more she felt connected to the people around her. For the first time, she began to open up to others—sharing her story, her pain, her journey. And in return, she found that others were willing to share their stories with her. It was in those moments of vulnerability that Violet realized how powerful feeling could be. It was through feeling that she was able to connect, to heal, and to grow.

One evening, as she sat by her window, watching the sunset, Violet reflected on how far she had come. She had spent most of her life numb, avoiding the pain because she thought it would destroy her. But now, she saw that the very thing she had feared the most was the thing that had saved her.

Feeling had given her back her life.

The numbness was gone, and in its place was a deep well of emotions—both painful and beautiful. And for the first time, Violet wasn't afraid to feel. She wasn't afraid to cry, to laugh, to love, and to grieve. She wasn't afraid to be fully alive.

As she watched the last rays of the sun dip below the horizon, she whispered a prayer of gratitude. She had been through the storm, through the darkness, and she had emerged on the other side. She had felt every moment of it, and she was stronger because of it.

For the first time in her life, Violet felt whole.

And that, she realized, was the true power of feeling.

Chapter 12: Neglect to Nurture

For years, Violet had been starved of the care and attention she so desperately needed. Her childhood had been marked by neglect—emotional, physical, and spiritual. The adults in her life had failed to protect her, failed to nurture her, and in turn, she had learned to neglect herself. The cycle of neglect continued into her adulthood, leaving her grasping for love and validation in all the wrong places.

But something was different now.

For the first time in her life, Violet was learning what it meant to nurture herself. It wasn't easy, and at first, it felt foreign, even uncomfortable. But she was determined. If she could break free from the chains of violence, shame, and self-sabotage, she could certainly learn to take care of herself in the way she always deserved.

Violet sat on the edge of her bed, holding a cup of tea in her hands. It was still early in the morning, and the sun was just beginning to rise, casting a warm, golden light through the window. She had started this new routine a few weeks ago—waking up early, sitting in stillness, and giving herself time to breathe before the chaos of the day began. It was a small thing, but for her, it felt monumental.

In the past, she would have rushed out of bed, barely giving herself time to think or reflect. But now, she was making a conscious effort to slow down, to be present, and to show herself the love and care she had been denied for so long.

Self-care, she realized, wasn't about luxury. It was about survival. It was about healing.

One of the first things she had learned in her journey of transformation was the importance of taking care of her body. For years, she had abused it—through unhealthy relationships, poor choices, and the lingering effects of her past trauma. But now, she was learning to listen to her body, to treat it with kindness.

She had started going for walks in the park, something she had never done before. There was something about being outside, surrounded by trees and flowers, that made her feel connected to the world around her. She would walk for miles, breathing in the fresh air, feeling the earth beneath her feet, and letting the peace of nature wash over her.

On these walks, she began to notice things she had never noticed before—the way the sunlight filtered through the leaves, the sound of birds singing, the feeling of the wind against her skin. These small moments of beauty reminded her that she was part of something bigger, that she was worthy of experiencing the beauty and peace she had been denied for so long.

But self-care wasn't just about the physical—it was about her spirit, too.

Violet had always struggled with her faith. She believed in God, but for so long, she had felt abandoned. How could a loving God have allowed her to suffer so much? How could He have watched as she was hurt, betrayed, and neglected?

It had taken her a long time to come to terms with those questions, and she still didn't have all the answers. But what she did know was that God hadn't abandoned her. He had been with her all along, even in the darkest moments, even when she couldn't feel Him. And now, as she sat in quiet reflection each morning, she could feel His presence more strongly than ever.

Her prayer life had deepened. No longer were her prayers just cries for help in moments of desperation. Now, they were conversations—honest, raw, and open. She thanked God for the strength He had given her, for the grace that had carried her through the storm, and for the opportunity to start again. And slowly, she began to feel the weight of her past lifting, replaced by a peace that only faith could bring.

One evening, Violet found herself back at the community center where she had once received help. But this time, she wasn't there as a participant—she was there as a leader.

The center had a support group for women who had experienced trauma, abuse, and neglect. For months, Violet had been attending the meetings, quietly listening to the stories of other women, feeling the comfort of knowing she wasn't alone in her pain. But tonight was different. Tonight, she had been asked to share her story.

She stood at the front of the room, her hands trembling slightly, but her voice steady. She told the women about her childhood, about the abuse she had endured, the neglect, and the violence. She spoke about the years of self-sabotage, the toxic relationships, and the anger that had consumed her. But then, she spoke about hope.

"I used to think I wasn't worthy of love," Violet said, her eyes scanning the room. "I thought that because no one took care of me, I didn't deserve to be cared for. But that's not true. We all deserve to be loved, to be nurtured, to be seen."

She paused, taking a deep breath. "I'm learning that now. I'm learning to love myself, to care for myself in the ways I should have been cared for as a child. It's not easy, and there are days when I still struggle. But I'm choosing to nurture myself, to give myself the grace and love that God has always offered me."

When she finished speaking, the room was silent for a moment, and then, one by one, the women began to clap. Some had tears in their eyes, others were smiling, but all of them were connected in that moment by the shared understanding of what it meant to survive.

Violet's journey of nurturing didn't stop with herself. As she grew stronger, she began to nurture others, too. She started creating art again, something she hadn't done since she was a child. Her paintings were raw, emotional, filled with the colors and images of her past, but also with the hope of her future.

She used her art as a form of expression, as a way to heal. But more than that, she used it as a way to connect with others. She began hosting small art workshops at the community center, teaching other women how to express their emotions through creativity. It wasn't about being perfect or creating something beautiful—it was about release, about letting go of the pain and allowing the art to speak.

As the months passed, Violet found herself surrounded by a community of people who cared for her and whom she cared for in return. She had finally learned to nurture herself, to heal the wounds of her past, and in doing so, she had created a life filled with love, faith, and purpose.

She wasn't the violent girl she had once been. She was Violet—a woman who had learned to bloom, even in the darkest of places.

And she knew that she would keep growing, keep nurturing, not just herself, but everyone around her. Because that's what grace does—it doesn't just heal; it spreads.

Chapter 13: Blooming in Grace

The transformation had been slow, but as Violet looked at herself in the mirror now, she could see it. She had become the person she never thought she could be—free from the chains of her past, no longer violent, no longer consumed by the weight of the "N" traits that once defined her.

Violet had bloomed.

It wasn't just that she had survived. Surviving, she realized, had been the easy part. Blooming—thriving—was what had taken real work. But now, she was thriving in ways that seemed unimaginable to the girl she had once been. She had become the person she had needed so desperately as a child: nurturing, forgiving, and filled with grace.

The morning sunlight streamed through the window as she sat in her studio, surrounded by the paintings and sketches that told the story of her journey. Her hands moved effortlessly across the canvas, painting soft violet flowers blooming against a backdrop of dark, swirling clouds. It was the perfect representation of her life—a reminder that beauty could grow even in the midst of chaos.

As she worked, her thoughts drifted to the people who had hurt her. Her grandfather. Her mother. The men who had stolen her innocence. She thought about the deep scars they had left on her heart and the years of anger and bitterness that had followed. There was a time when she believed she would never be able to forgive them.

But something had changed.

Forgiveness, she realized, wasn't about letting them off the hook. It wasn't about excusing what they had done. Forgiveness was about freeing herself from the burden of their actions. It was about letting go of the hatred and anger that had kept her trapped in the past. It was about reclaiming her power.

Violet had begun to forgive, one step at a time.

The first person she had forgiven was herself.

For years, she had carried the weight of shame, believing that somehow, she was to blame for the things that had happened to her. She blamed herself for not fighting harder, for not being strong enough to escape, for becoming the very thing she had despised. But now, she understood that none of it had been her fault. She had been a child, doing her best to survive in a world that had been cruel and unkind.

And so, she had offered herself grace.

She had begun to nurture her own heart, forgiving herself for the mistakes she had made, for the times she had hurt others, and for the years she had spent living in darkness. It hadn't been easy, and there were days when the old shame would creep back in, whispering lies in her ear. But each time, she would remind herself that she was not the girl she used to be. She was Violet now—a woman who had chosen love over hate, grace over bitterness.

The next person she had forgiven was her mother.

For so many years, Violet had harbored deep resentment towards the woman who had brought her into the world but had failed to protect her. Her mother's schizophrenia had been a cruel thief, stealing her away from Violet when she had needed her the most. And in her illness, her mother had caused so much pain—neglect, abuse, and betrayal.

But as Violet grew stronger in her own healing, she began to see her mother through different eyes. She saw her not as the villain of her story, but as a broken woman, fighting demons of her own. Her mother had been a victim too—of mental illness, of trauma, of a world that hadn't shown her the love and care she needed. In forgiving her mother, Violet wasn't condoning what had happened, but she was choosing to see the humanity in her.

One afternoon, Violet had written her mother a letter. She hadn't known where to send it, and maybe it didn't matter. The act of writing it had been enough. In the letter, she told her mother about the life she had built, about the healing she had found, and about the love she had for her, despite everything.

"I forgive you, Mom," she had written. "I forgive you for the pain, for the mistakes, for the things you couldn't control. I choose to love you, and I choose to let go of the anger I've carried for so long."

The weight that lifted off her shoulders after writing that letter was indescribable. For the first time in her life, Violet felt free.

But perhaps the hardest forgiveness had been for her grandfather.

He had been the source of so much of her pain—the man who had stolen her childhood, who had betrayed her trust in the most horrific ways. For years, Violet had fantasized about getting revenge, about making him feel the same pain he had inflicted on her. But now, she understood that revenge wouldn't heal her. Only grace could do that.

In her heart, she forgave him.

It wasn't about making peace with what he had done. Some things were unforgivable. But it was about releasing herself from the prison of hatred and anger she had built around her heart. She forgave him not for his sake, but for her own.

In forgiving her grandfather, Violet took back the power he had stolen from her. She was no longer his victim. She was no longer defined by what had happened to her. She was free.

Violet stood in front of a group of women at the community center, sharing her story. These were women who had been through their own storms—survivors of abuse, addiction, and trauma. Some of them were just beginning their journey of healing, while others, like Violet, were further along the path.

"As long as you hold onto the pain," Violet said, her voice steady and strong, "it will keep you trapped. But when you choose grace—when you choose to forgive—you set yourself free. It doesn't mean forgetting, and it doesn't mean excusing what happened. But it does mean that you get to take back control of your life."

She looked around the room, meeting the eyes of each woman. "You have the power to bloom, even in the darkest places. You are more than what happened to you. You are more than the names they called you. You are beautiful. You are strong. And you deserve to be free."

The room was silent for a moment, and then one of the women raised her hand. "How do you forgive?" she asked, her voice trembling. "How do you let go of all the anger?"

Violet smiled softly. "It's not easy," she said. "It takes time, and it takes faith. But when you trust that you are worthy of grace—that you are worthy of healing—it gets easier. One day at a time, one step at a time, you let go. And when you do, you'll feel lighter. You'll feel free."

Violet left the community center that evening, feeling a deep sense of peace. She had come so far from the girl she had once been. The girl who had been called Ugly, Stupid, and Floozy. The girl who had lived in darkness, trapped by violence and shame.

She was Violet now. A woman who had bloomed in grace. A woman who had forgiven, who had let go, and who was thriving.

As she walked through the park, the evening sun casting a warm glow over the trees, she smiled to herself. She had done it. She had removed the "N." She had chosen grace.

And now, she was free to bloom.

Chapter 14: Sharing the Story

The first time Violet stepped up to the pulpit, her heart raced in her chest. She had shared her story before, but never in a setting like this. The church pews were filled with people—some survivors of their own traumas, some just curious about the woman who had come through so much darkness and was now standing in the light. She took a deep breath, looked out at the faces watching her, and began.

"My name is Violet," she said, her voice steady. "But I wasn't always Violet. For a long time, I was Violent. I was angry. I was hurt. I was trapped in a cycle of pain that felt impossible to escape. But today, I stand before you, not as the girl I used to be, but as the woman God helped me become. I want to share with you how God removed the 'N' from my life, how I went from being Violent to being Violet."

The first time Violet had spoken publicly about her journey, it was in a small room at the local community center. The group had been intimate—just a handful of women who had gathered for a support group meeting. She had shared her story hesitantly at first, unsure of how much to reveal, unsure of how it would be received. But as she spoke, she realized that her story wasn't just hers anymore. It was a story that others needed to hear, a story that could help others heal just as she had.

After that, the invitations began to come in. Churches, rehabilitation centers, even prisons. People wanted to hear how Violet had transformed her life, how she had shed the destructive "N" traits that had once defined her. Her story wasn't just about surviving trauma—it was about thriving after trauma. It was about showing others that they too could remove the "N" from their own lives.

At the church, Violet spoke with clarity and conviction, her words reaching every corner of the room. She told them about her childhood, the labels she had been given—Ugly, Stupid, Floozy—and how those labels had become her identity for so long. She spoke about the abuse she had endured, about how the violent storm of her past had shaped her into someone who hurt others, just as she had been hurt.

But then she told them about the moment everything changed. The moment when God whispered to her, telling her that she didn't have to be violent, that she didn't have to carry the "N." She shared how she had started the painful but necessary work of transformation—removing the traits of Narcissism, Neglect, Negativity, and

Numbing from her life, and replacing them with love, grace, and forgiveness.

"I didn't think I was worthy of love," Violet said, her voice soft but firm. "I thought I was too broken, too far gone. But God showed me that I wasn't broken—I was just blooming. He showed me that the things I had been through didn't define me. He showed me that I could be made new, that I could be Violet."

After her talk, people came up to her one by one. Some thanked her for her bravery, some asked her how they could begin their own transformation, and others simply hugged her, tears in their eyes, grateful for the hope her story had given them. In those moments, Violet knew that every tear, every scar, every painful memory had been worth it if it meant she could help others find their way to healing.

Violet wasn't just sharing her story—she was giving people permission to confront their own pasts, to face their own storms, and to believe that they, too, could transform. She was showing them that their pain didn't have to define them, that they could remove the "N" and step into the fullness of who they were meant to be.

It wasn't long before Violet was traveling to different cities, speaking at prisons, rehabilitation centers, and churches all over the country. Each place she visited was different, but the people she met were always the same—they were searching for hope, for a way out of the darkness, for a reason to believe that they could be something more than the sum of their past mistakes.

In the prisons, Violet saw the same hopelessness she had once felt. She saw women who had been beaten down by life, who had turned to violence and crime because they didn't know any other way. But she also saw something else—she saw the spark of possibility in their eyes when she told them her story. She saw the shift in their posture when she spoke about how God had removed the "N" from her life, about how they could remove it from theirs too.

"You are not the worst thing that's ever happened to you," Violet would tell them. "You are not the mistakes you've made. You are more than your past. God sees you. He sees the beautiful, blooming soul inside of you, and He wants to help you set it free."

In rehabilitation centers, Violet spoke to people who were battling addiction, just as she had battled her own demons. She knew what it felt like to numb the pain with substances, with toxic relationships, with anything that would make her forget who she was. But she also knew the freedom that came from finally allowing herself to feel, to grieve, to heal.

"I know it's hard," she told them. "But you are worth the fight. You are worth the effort it takes to heal. God has a plan for your life, and it's bigger than the pain you're feeling right now. He can remove the 'N'—the Negativity, the Narcotic Dependence, the Numbing—and replace it with something beautiful. You can bloom."

Everywhere Violet went, her story made an impact. People who had felt lost, who had believed that they were too damaged to ever change, began to see the possibility of transformation. They began to believe that they could bloom just like Violet had.

And Violet's own life continued to blossom. She found joy in helping others, in sharing the message of grace and healing that had changed her own life. She no longer carried the weight of her past, no longer felt defined by the violence that had once consumed her. Instead, she felt empowered by her story, knowing that it was a tool for helping others transform their lives.

One day, after speaking at a women's prison, a young woman approached Violet. She was hesitant, unsure of herself, but there was something in her eyes—a spark of hope.

"How did you know it was time to change?" the woman asked.

Violet smiled gently. "I didn't," she said. "I just knew that I couldn't keep living the way I had been. I knew that if I didn't change, I would destroy myself. But even then, it wasn't me who did the changing. It was God. He took the broken pieces of my life and made something beautiful out of them. And He can do the same for you."

The woman nodded, her eyes filling with tears. "I want to change," she whispered.

Violet placed a hand on her shoulder. "You can," she said. "You already have. The moment you decided you wanted something different, you started your journey. God will guide you the rest of the way."

As Violet left the prison that day, she felt a deep sense of peace. She had found her purpose. Her past no longer controlled her—it empowered her to help others. She had gone from being Violent to being Violet, and now she was helping others do the same.

Her story was no longer just her own. It was a beacon of hope, a light in the darkness, a reminder that no matter how broken someone might feel, they could always bloom. And as long as there were people who needed to hear that message, Violet would continue to share it.

Chapter 15: Violet's Legacy

Violet stood at the front of the room, the warm glow of the afternoon sun casting a soft light on her face. The room was filled with people—survivors, supporters, and curious onlookers—all drawn together by one thing: hope. And hope was something Violet knew intimately. It had taken years to understand it, to feel it, to live it. But now, she was its embodiment.

As she gazed out at the faces before her, Violet felt an overwhelming sense of gratitude. She had spent so long believing she wasn't worthy of love, that she was broken beyond repair. But God had shown her that her cracks were not flaws—they were the spaces where the light could enter. And now, she was a vessel of that light, shining it on others who needed it just as much as she once had.

Violet's new mission in life was clear: to help others bloom, just as she had. Whether through her organization, Color Your Story Onto Mine, or the workshops and talks she gave, Violet was determined to make sure no one ever felt as trapped, as hopeless, as she had. She had gone from being Violent to being Violet, and now it was her turn to guide others on their own journey of transformation.

The initiative had started small—a few workshops in local churches and community centers. But as word spread, so did the reach of Color Your Story Onto Mine. Soon, Violet was working with women in prisons, survivors of abuse, and even individuals in behavioral health centers. Her message was simple but profound: "You can remove the 'N' from your life. You can go from broken to blooming."

The impact of her work was palpable. Letters poured in from women who had attended her talks, telling her how her story had changed their lives. They wrote about how they had begun to confront their own "N" traits—negativity, narcissism, numbing—and how they were learning to replace those traits with grace, self-compassion, and love.

"Dear Violet," one letter read, "Your story made me realize that I've been living in my own storm for years. I thought the storm defined me, but now I see that I have the power to change. I'm not there yet, but for the first time, I believe it's possible. Thank you for showing me that I can bloom, too."

Violet smiled as she read the letter. It was moments like this that reminded her why she did what she did. Every letter, every conversation, every woman who stood a little taller after hearing her story—this was her legacy. She had once been a victim of violence, of abuse, of a broken system. But now, she was a beacon of healing, a living testament to the power of transformation.

Color Your Story Onto Mine had grown into something larger than Violet ever imagined. What had once been a personal mission to heal herself had blossomed into a movement. The organization now offered art therapy, emotional literacy workshops, and trauma recovery programs in partnership with local churches, correctional facilities, and community outreach centers. Violet had even begun to train other survivors to become mentors and facilitators, helping them share their own stories of transformation.

But for Violet, it wasn't about the accolades or the growing success of her organization. It was about the individual lives that were being touched, one person at a time. It was about the women who came up to her after a workshop, tears in their eyes, and told her, "Because of you, I believe I can heal."

One evening, after a particularly moving workshop at a women's prison, Violet sat alone in the quiet of her small office. She looked at the painting that hung on the wall—a simple violet flower, blooming against a backdrop of dark, stormy clouds. It was the first piece of art she had created after her transformation, a symbol of everything she had gone through and everything she had become.

As she traced the petals of the flower with her eyes, Violet thought about her journey. She had been through hell and back. She had been broken, battered, and bruised. But she had also been healed, restored, and renewed. And now, she was blooming—just as God had promised she would.

She thought about her daughter, her family, and the many people who had come into her life over the years. She had hurt many of them in her darkest moments, but she had also healed those relationships, one by one. It hadn't been easy, and the process of forgiveness—of herself and others—had taken time. But now, she stood on the other side of it, free from the weight of her past.

Violet's legacy was not one of violence. It was one of healing, of grace, of transformation. And she knew that her work was far from over. There were still so many people out there who needed to hear her story, who needed to know that change was possible, that they could remove the "N" and step into the fullness of who they were meant to be.

As she closed her eyes, a deep sense of peace washed over her. She had finally found her purpose. She had been given the gift of healing, and now she was sharing that gift with the world. Her story, once a source of pain and shame, had become a tool of empowerment and hope.

In the years that followed, Violet's work continued to grow. She began to collaborate with other organizations, expanding the reach of Color Your Story Onto Mine to other states and even other countries. But no matter how large her platform became, Violet remained grounded in her mission: to help others bloom.

Her story became a beacon of hope, not just for survivors of trauma, but for anyone who had ever felt trapped in the storm of their own life. She showed them that the storm didn't have to define them—that they could bloom, even in the rain.

And so, as Violet stood before a group of women at yet another workshop, she smiled softly. "My name is Violet," she said, her voice steady and sure. "And I'm here to tell you that no matter what you've been through, no matter how broken you feel, you can bloom. You can remove the 'N' from your life. You can be whole. You can be free."

The room was silent for a moment, and then one by one, the women began to nod. They understood. They believed.

And in that moment, Violet knew that her legacy was secure. She had bloomed, and now she was helping others do the same.

Her journey from violent to Violet was complete, and she was ready to continue sharing her story—her legacy—for as long as the world needed to hear it.

Epilogue

Violet stood in the garden she had planted, surrounded by blooming flowers of every color, but the violets held a special place in her heart. As she watched the wind gently sway their delicate petals, she reflected on the journey that had brought her to this moment. It had not been easy. The road from "violent" to "Violet" had been long, painful, and full of setbacks. But every step had been necessary.

There was still work to do. Healing, she realized, was a lifelong process. But she no longer lived in fear or anger. She no longer carried the "N" traits that had once chained her to her past. She was free. And in that freedom, she had found her true purpose—to share her story, to help others remove their own burdens, and to remind them that they, too, could bloom in the light of God's grace.

As she walked through the garden, her hand brushing against the violets, she smiled. She was no longer the girl trapped in a storm. She was Violet, fully bloomed.

Afterword

As I reflect on the journey that led to the creation of From Violent to Violet: God Removed the 'N', I find myself filled with gratitude for the transformation that has taken place, not just in my life but in the lives of those who have walked this path with me. Writing this book was both a challenge and a privilege, allowing me to revisit the darkest corners of my past while celebrating the beauty that emerged from the ashes.

My hope for you, the reader, is that this book has stirred something deep within—a recognition that transformation is possible, no matter how broken or bruised you feel. The road to healing is not easy, and it requires faith, resilience, and the willingness to confront the very things that have caused us pain. But it is in this confrontation that we find the grace to heal and the strength to move forward.

This book is not the end of my journey; rather, it marks a new beginning, one in which I continue to share my story and help others navigate their own path to healing. The work of removing the destructive "N" traits is ongoing, but with each step, I see more clearly the person God intended me to be. My prayer is that you too will embark on your own journey of transformation, letting go of the traits that no longer serve you and embracing the beauty and strength that lies within.

Thank you for walking with me through these pages. May you find healing, hope, and the courage to bloom, just as I have.

Appendix

This section includes some supplementary material that may be useful for readers who wish to dive deeper into the themes and practices discussed throughout the book:

1. Scripture References:
   - Isaiah 61:3 — "To appoint unto them that mourn in Zion, to give unto them beauty for ashes, the oil of joy for mourning, the garment of praise for the spirit of heaviness."
   - Romans 12:2 — "Do not conform to the pattern of this world, but be transformed by the renewing of your mind."
   - Psalm 34:18 — "The Lord is close to the brokenhearted and saves those who are crushed in spirit."

2. Emotional Literacy Prompts:
   - What are the emotions I feel most often, and how do they affect my actions?
   - How can I express emotions through art or journaling in a way that feels healing?

3. Artistic Healing Exercises:
   - Create a self-portrait that represents both the person you were and the person you are becoming.
   - Use colors to represent emotions you feel when thinking about past trauma or healing.

Glossary

Emotional Literacy: The ability to recognize, understand, and express one's emotions in a healthy way.

Faith-Based Healing: A process of healing that centers around spiritual beliefs and practices, often involving prayer, scripture, and trust in a higher power.

Nonviolent Communication: A communication method developed by Marshall Rosenberg that focuses on empathetic listening, expressing feelings and needs clearly, and avoiding conflict escalation.

Trauma-Informed Care: An approach to care that acknowledges the widespread impact of trauma and the potential paths for recovery, emphasizing safety, trustworthiness, and empowerment.

Violet: In this context, Violet is both the name the author claims after her transformation and a symbol of growth, beauty, and grace emerging from hardship.

Bibliography

Though much of this book draws from personal experience and faith-based inspiration, I've also referenced and been influenced by numerous texts, scriptures, and studies that have shaped my understanding of trauma, healing, and transformation. Below are key sources that have contributed to the themes explored in From Violent to Violet: God Removed the 'N':

1. Rosenberg, Marshall B. Nonviolent Communication: A Language of Life. PuddleDancer Press, 2003.
2. Bessel van der Kolk, M.D. The Body Keeps the Score: Brain, Mind, and Body in the Healing of Trauma. Penguin Books, 2015.
3. The Holy Bible, various translations, specifically:
   - New International Version (NIV)
   - King James Version (KJV)
   - New Living Translation (NLT)
4. Nouwen, Henri J. M. The Wounded Healer: Ministry in Contemporary Society. Image Books, 1979.
5. Brown, Brené. The Gifts of Imperfection: Let Go of Who You Think You're Supposed to Be

and Embrace Who You Are. Hazelden
Publishing, 2010.
6. Herman, Judith L. Trauma and Recovery:
The Aftermath of Violence—from Domestic
Abuse to Political Terror. Basic Books, 1997.

For further resources on emotional literacy, trauma-informed care, and faith-based healing, please visit the Color Your Story Onto Mine website at https://coloryourstoryontomine.com/

If you are interested in attending workshops or learning more about the Color Your Story Onto Mine curriculum, please reach out via the contact page on the website.

Also by Violet Newborn:
- Only God Can Grow a Violet Out of a Pile of Dirt
- Art for Healing: How Creative Expression Transformed My Journey (coming soon)

Author Bio:
Violet Newborn is a trauma survivor, artist, and the founder of Color Your Story Onto Mine, a nonprofit organization dedicated to healing through creative expression. As a Certified Peer Recovery Specialist and teaching artist, Violet has led workshops and programs to help individuals find their voice and transform their pain into purpose. She is passionate about using faith and art to promote healing in underserved communities, particularly for African-American, Native and Indengious women and girls and those who identify as such. From Violent to Violet is her second book, following Only God Can Grow A Violet Out of a Pile of Dirt.

Made in the USA
Columbia, SC
29 October 2024

45001759R00059